MW01098204

# Bits & Pieces Quilt

### Anne Dease

a Quilt in a Day® publication

*For my best friend Jim, and our children Jonathan and Meghan. Your love, patience and support make my dreams possible.*

*And to my parents, Theodore and Nellie Van Klaveren, who taught me that dreams do come true…if you work hard enough to achieve them.*

Published by Quilt in a Day, Inc.

1955 Diamond Street, San Marcos, CA 92069

Copyright 1994 by Anne Dease

First Printing March, 1994

ISBN 0-922705-48-8

Editor  Eleanor Burns

Art Direction Merritt Voigtlander

Photography Wayne Norton

Printed in the United States of America on recycled paper.  All rights reserved.  No part of this material may be reproduced in any form or by any electronic or mechanical means, including information storage and retrieval systems, without permission in writing from the author.

# Contents

# Introduction

I can't remember a time when I wasn't interested in quilts. To me they always seemed to express a happy, safe and cozy home.

Unfortunately, I wasn't blessed with a trunk full of quilts inherited from pioneer relatives. My parents were certainly "modern" pioneers. They escaped the ravages of starvation and their bombed out city of Rotterdam, Holland, and came to this country in search of hope and a future for their children. They came with very little in material goods, but created a home rich in comfort and love. From my mother I learned that "much can be made with little."

When it came time to establish our own home, I found strength in what my mother had shared with me. Like many families today, our lives were one in constant motion. In the first 15 years of our marriage, Jim, the children and I, settled in six different homes from coast to coast, and points in between. Jim faced the challenges of his career, while I was responsible for making each home a loving and welcoming place.

Nothing seemed as "settling" as to decorate our home in quilts. With little knowledge, but a lot of desire, I entered my first quilt shop. The book that the helpful clerk gave to me was written by Eleanor Burns. I was fascinated that I could make a "Quilt in a Day." What could be better for a busy mom who was called upon to decorate a new home every few years!

As I look at my collection of quilts, I think about the "Bits & Pieces" that I have put into each one. I remember places that we have been and friends that we have made. While I will always envy people who are blessed with an abundance of heirloom quilts, I am most proud that I have begun my own heritage of quiltmaking.

I hope you will surround yourself with the comfort of quilts and that in each one you place "bits and pieces" of life's most wonderful memories. And remember, too, that home is not always just a place, but a feeling you carry in your hearts forever.

# Supplies

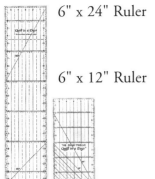

6" x 24" Ruler

6" x 12" Ruler

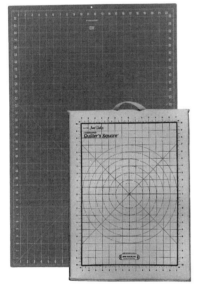

12½" Square Up Ruler

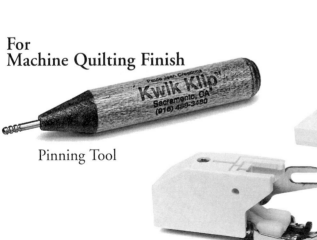

100% Cotton Fabric, at least 42 inches wide

Sewing machine with ¼" presser foot

Serger (optional)

Magnetic Seam Guide

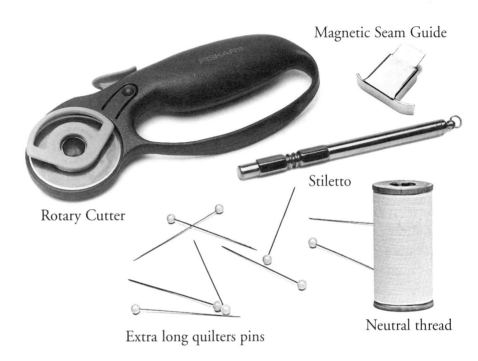

Rotary Cutter

Stiletto

Extra long quilters pins

Neutral thread

Gridded pressing mat

Gridded Cutting Mat 24" x 36"

Embroidery Floss
for Quick Turn Finish

**For
Machine Quilting Finish**

Pinning Tool

Walking Foot

Darning Foot
or
Spring Needle

Monofilament Nylon Thread

Fabric Marker

# Planning Your Fabrics

The "Bits & Pieces" quilt is very similar to the Irish Chain. The difference is in the construction and use of multi fabrics that give the block its scrap look. When choosing your fabrics, begin by choosing that one fabric that "must" be in your quilt. This is your inspiration fabric. Take this inspiration fabric and then choose additional fabrics of different print scales and values that compliment your original choice. Be creative in your choices.

It is important that your chain fabrics have strong contrast with your background fabrics. If you choose a light background fabric, be sure that your chain fabrics are of

medium or dark values. The opposite is true if you choose a dark background. Fabrics that are directional, or plaid, can be used, but it should be understood that these fabrics will be turned within the design of the quilt. This can enhance the scrap look of the quilt. If you want your quilt to look less random, choose fabrics that are nondirectional. A paste-up will be very helpful to determine your design. **Do not skip this important step.**

Variations of the pattern are possible and are encouraged. If you want a more "scrappy" look to your quilt, cut the same number of strips, choosing fabrics that are all different. For example, the baby quilt calls for background fabric and thirteen additional strips, some of which are used more than once. You can substitute by choosing thirteen different strips, giving less repeat and a more "scrappy" appearance in your quilt.

As you can see, the variations are as multiple as the quilt maker. This quilt gives you a good opportunity to be surprised by the possibilities of combining color and design. I hope you enjoy this challenge as much as I have.

# Paste Up Sheet

Paste fabric on small squares
and on corresponding positions
in larger block. Use fabrics A, C,
E, G and I once. Use B, D, F
and H twice.

**A**

**B**

**C**

**D**

**E**

**F**

**G**

**H**

**I**

| | | | | |
|---|---|---|---|---|
| **Row 1** | A | B | | |
| **Row 2** | B | C | D | |
| **Row 3** | | D | E | F |
| **Row 4** | | | F | G  H |
| **Row 5** | | | | H  I |

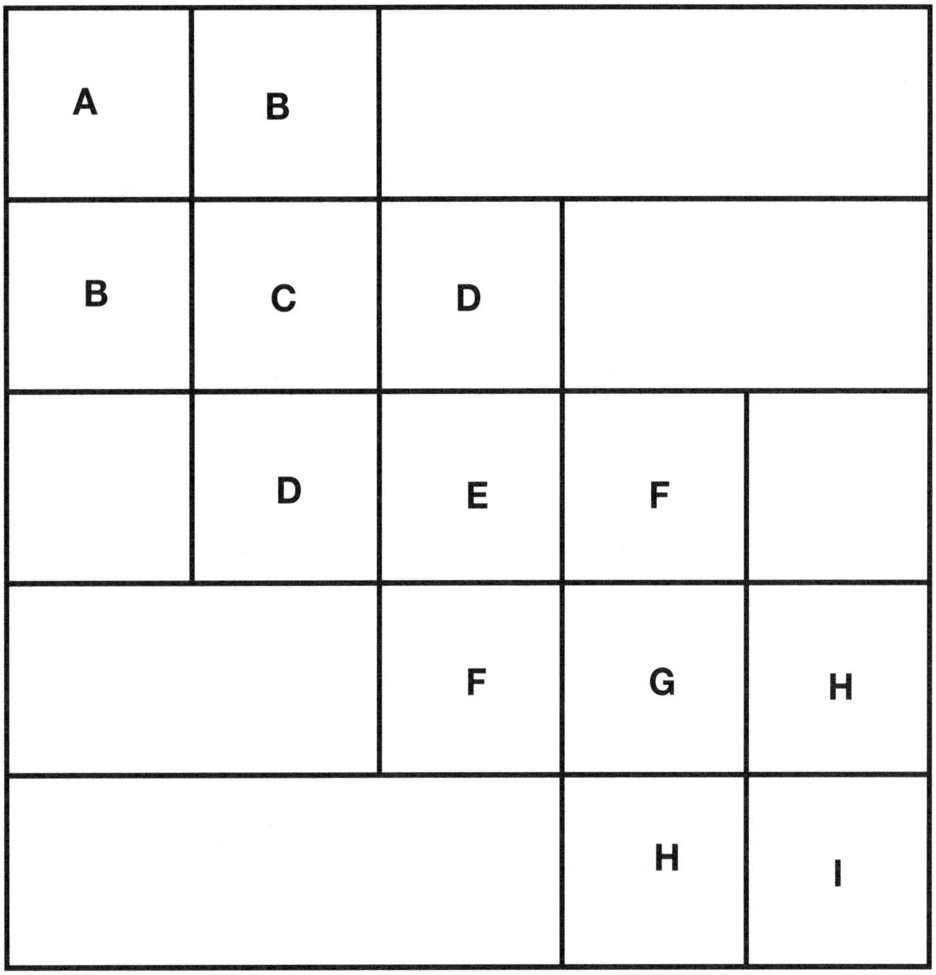

Block size: Approximately 10 ½″ unfinished, 10" finished.

**Background**

**Do <u>NOT</u> Skip this Important Step!**

# Techniques

## Cutting Strips

Make a nick on the edge and tear from selvage to selvage to put the fabric on the straight-of-the-grain.

Fold the fabric in half, matching the torn straight edge thread to thread. It is often impossible to match the selvages.

Line up the torn edge of fabric on the gridded cutting mat with the left edge extended slightly to the left of zero.

Line up the 6" by 24" ruler on zero. Reverse this procedure if you are left-handed.

Spread the fingers of your left hand to hold the ruler firmly. With the rotary cutter in your right hand, begin cutting with the blade off the fabric on the mat. Put all your strength into the rotary cutter as you cut away from you, and trim the torn, ragged edge.

Lift, and move your ruler over until it lines up with the size of the strip that your are cutting. Cut the strip carefully and accurately.

Lift the ruler, move it, and line it up with the correct ruler width for your next strip. Repeat, cutting as many strips as indicated for your particular size quilt.

After cutting several strips, unfold and check to see that the strip is straight. If the strip is not straight, tear your fabric to put it on the straight-of-grain and begin again.

## Labeling the Strips

It is very important to mark your fabrics in the chain from A to I.

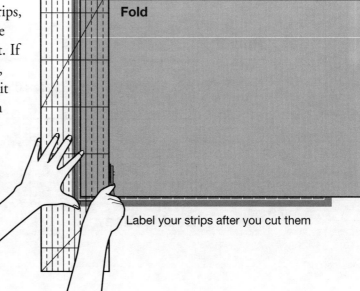

Label your strips after you cut them

# Sewing

The width of the presser foot usually determines the seam allowance. Line the edges of the fabric with the edge of the presser foot and sew a few stitches. Measure the seam allowance. If it is ¼", a magnetic seam guide placed on the metal throat plate against the presser foot will assure a consistent ¼" seam. If the measurement is less than ¼", place the magnetic seam guide at a slight distance from the presser foot. A magnetic seam guide is not recommended for use with a computerized machine.

## Seam Allowance for Conventional Sewing Machine

Sew an accurate and consistent ¼" seam allowance throughout the sewing of the quilt. Do not change machines in the middle of making the quilt, because a consistent seam allowance is crucial.

When sewing be sure to use a small stitch, at least 15 stitches to the inch. This eliminates the need to backstitch.

## Seam Allowance for a Serger

"Bits & Pieces" can be made entirely on a conventional sewing machine. However, to speed the quilt making process, a serger can be used when making the top, as well as for a Quick Turn and Tie finish. A conventional machine is needed for a Machine Quilting and Binding finish.

A five thread serger with a chain stitch and an overcast stitch is preferred. If available, use the serger fabric guide attachment, and make the seam adjustment by moving the guide. Do not let the serger knife trim the edges. If a guide attachment is not available, stick a piece of moleskin on the serger so the seam is ¼".

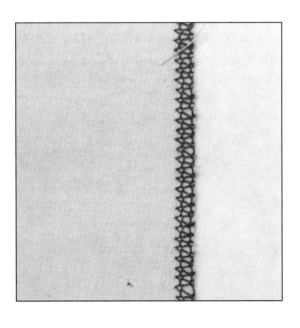

## Assembly-line Sewing

This method saves time and thread by sewing a pair and butting on other pairs without cutting the thread until you are finished sewing. Assembly-line sewing isn't recommended with large or heavy pieces because the weight tends to cause pulling which results in crooked seams.

A stiletto is helpful to direct the seam allowance while assembly-line sewing.

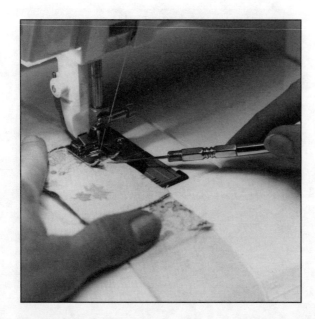

# Pressing

## Pressing to "Set and Direct the Seam Allowance"

Throughout the construction, it is important to "set the seams" and then press the seam allowances in a given direction. To insure that the pieces have locking seams, do not use the common practice of pressing seams toward the darker side.

## "Set the Seam"

Strips or pairs of strips are sewn right sides together.

Before opening, lay the sewn strips on the gridded pressing mat with a designated strip on the top. Lightly press the strips to "set the seam" as they lie right sides together.

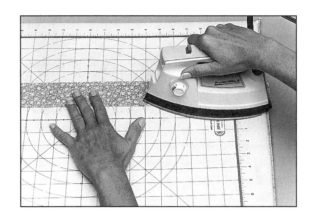

## "Direct the Seam Allowance"

Lift the upper strip and press toward the fold. The seam allowance will naturally fall behind the upper strip. Make sure there are no folds at the seam line.

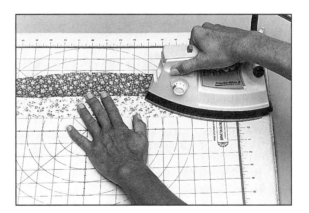

## "Press the Reverse Side"

Turn the strips over. Press the reverse and check that the seams are pressed in the right direction.

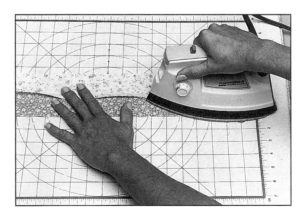

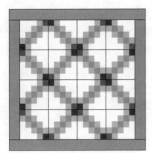

# Baby Quilt

Cut all strips selvage to selvage.

*16 blocks*

*4 blocks by 4 blocks down*

*Approximate finished size: 48" x 48"*

## Blocks    *Chain Fabrics A, C, E, G and I run down the center of the chain.*

| Chain Fabrics | Yardage | 2½" Strips |
|---|---|---|
| A | ⅛ yd | 1 |
| B | ¼ yd | 2 |
| C | ⅛ yd | 1 |
| D | ¼ yd | 2 |
| E | ⅛ yd | 1 |
| F | ¼ yd | 2 |
| G | ⅛ yd | 1 |
| H | ¼ yd | 2 |
| I | ⅛ yd | 1 |

| Background Fabric | Yardage | Background Strips |
|---|---|---|
| | 1 ¼ yds | Cut (2) 3" wide strips |
| | | Cut (2) 5" wide strips |
| | | Cut (2) 7" wide strips |

## Borders and Finishing

| | Yardage | Strips |
|---|---|---|
| First Border | ¾ yd | (5) 4 ½" wide strips |
| Backing | 3 yds | Cut 2 equal pieces & seam |
| Bonded Batting | 52" x 52" | |
| Binding | ⅔ yd | (5) 3 ½" wide strips |

# Lap Quilt

Cut all strips selvage to selvage.

*24 blocks*

*4 blocks by 6 blocks down*

*Approximate finished size: 54" x 73"*

## Blocks
*Chain Fabrics A, C, E, G and I run down the center of the chain.*

| Chain Fabrics | Yardage | 2½" Strips |
|---|---|---|
| A | ¼ yd | 2 |
| B | ⅜ yd | 4 |
| C | ¼ yd | 2 |
| D | ⅜ yd | 4 |
| E | ¼ yd | 2 |
| F | ⅜ yd | 4 |
| G | ¼ yd | 2 |
| H | ⅜ yd | 4 |
| I | ¼ yd | 2 |

| Background Fabric | Yardage | Background Strips |
|---|---|---|
| | 2 yds | Cut (4) 3" wide strips |
| | | Cut (4) 5" wide strips |
| | | Cut (4) 7" wide strips |

## Borders and Finishing

| | Yardage | Strips |
|---|---|---|
| First Border | ¾ yd | (6) 3 ½" wide strips |
| Second Border | 1 ⅜ yds | (8) 5 ½" wide strips |
| Backing | 4 ¼ yds | Cut 2 equal pieces & seam |
| Bonded Batting | 59" x 78" | |
| Binding | ⅞ yd | (7) 3 ½" wide strips |

# Twin Quilt

Cut all strips selvage to selvage.

*40 blocks*

*5 blocks by 8 blocks down*

*Approximate finished size:  72" x 100"*

## Blocks    *Chain Fabrics A, C, E, G and I run down the center of the chain.*

| Chain Fabrics | Yardage | 2½" Strips |
|---|---|---|
| A | ⅓ yd | 3 |
| B | ⅝ yd | 6 |
| C | ⅓ yd | 3 |
| D | ⅝ yd | 6 |
| E | ⅓ yd | 3 |
| F | ⅝ yd | 6 |
| G | ⅓ yd | 3 |
| H | ⅝ yd | 6 |
| I | ⅓ yd | 3 |

| Background Fabric | Yardage | Background Strips |
|---|---|---|
| | 2 ¾ yds | Cut (6) 3" wide strips |
| | | Cut (6) 5" wide strips |
| | | Cut (6) 7" wide strips |

## Borders and Finishing

| | Yardage | Strips |
|---|---|---|
| First Border | 1 yd | (8) 3 ½" wide strips |
| Second Border | 1 ⅜ yds | (10) 4 ½" wide strips |
| Third Border | 1 ⅞ yds | (11) 5 ½" wide strips |
| Backing | 6 yds | Cut 2 equal pieces & seam |
| Bonded Batting | 76" x 104" | |
| Binding | ⅞ yd | (9) 3 ½" wide strips |

# Double Quilt

Cut all strips selvage to selvage.

*48 blocks*

*6 blocks by 8 blocks down*

*Approximate finished size: 75" x 94"*

---

**Blocks**   *Chain Fabrics A, C, E, G and I run down the center of the chain.*

| Chain Fabrics | Yardage | 2½" Strips |
|---|---|---|
| A | ⅜ yd | 3 |
| B | ⅝ yd | 6 |
| C | ⅜ yd | 3 |
| D | ⅝ yd | 6 |
| E | ⅜ yd | 3 |
| F | ⅝ yd | 6 |
| G | ⅜ yd | 3 |
| H | ⅝ yd | 6 |
| I | ⅜ yd | 3 |

| Background Fabric | Yardage | Background Strips |
|---|---|---|
| | 3 ½ yds | Cut (6) 3" wide strips |
| | | Cut (6) 5" wide strips |
| | | Cut (6) 7" wide strips |

## Borders and Finishing

| | Yardage | Strips |
|---|---|---|
| First Border | 1 yd | (8) 3 ½" wide strips |
| Second Border | 1 ⅞ yds | (9) 6 ½" wide strips |
| Backing | 6 yds | Cut 2 equal pieces & seam |
| Bonded Batting | 79" x 99" | |
| Binding | 1 yd | (9) 3 ½" wide strips |

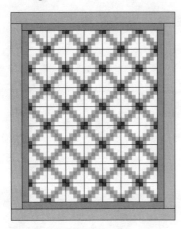

# Queen Quilt

Cut all strips selvage to selvage.

*63 blocks*

*7 blocks by 9 blocks down*

*Approximate finished size:  84" x 103"*

## Blocks   *Chain Fabrics A, C, E, G and I run down the center of the chain.*

| Chain Fabrics | Yardage | 2½" Strips |
|---|---|---|
| A | ½ yd | 4 |
| B | ⅞ yd | 8 |
| C | ½ yd | 4 |
| D | ⅞ yd | 8 |
| E | ½ yd | 4 |
| F | ⅞ yd | 8 |
| G | ½ yd | 4 |
| H | ⅞ yd | 8 |
| I | ½ yd | 4 |

| Background Fabric | Yardage | Background Strips |
|---|---|---|
| | 4 ⅜ yds | Cut (8) 3" wide strips |
| | | Cut (8) 5" wide strips |
| | | Cut (8) 7" wide strips |

## Borders and Finishing

| | Yardage | Strips |
|---|---|---|
| First Border | 1 ⅛ yds | (10) 3 ½" wide strips |
| Second Border | 2 ⅛ yds | (12) 5 ½" wide strips |
| Backing | 9 ½ yds | Cut 3 equal pieces & seam |
| Bonded Batting | 90" x 108" | |
| Binding | 1 ¼ yds | (12) 3 ½" wide strips |

# King Quilt

Cut all strips selvage to selvage.

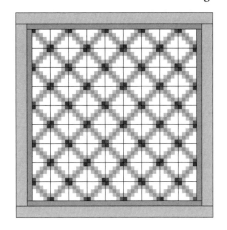

*81 blocks*

*9 blocks by 9 blocks down*

*Approximate finished size: 106" x 106"*

## Blocks   *Chain Fabrics A, C, E, G and I run down the center of the chain.*

| Chain Fabrics | Yardage | 2½" Strips |
|---|---|---|
| A | ½ yd | 6 |
| B | 1 yd | 12 |
| C | ½ yd | 6 |
| D | 1 yd | 12 |
| E | ½ yd | 6 |
| F | 1 yd | 12 |
| G | ½ yd | 6 |
| H | 1 yd | 12 |
| I | ½ yd | 6 |

| Background Fabric | Yardage | Background Strips |
|---|---|---|
| | 5¼ yds | Cut (12) 3" wide strips |
| | | Cut (12) 5" wide strips |
| | | Cut (12) 7" wide strips |

## Borders and Finishing

| | Yardage | Strips |
|---|---|---|
| First Border | 1⅛ yds | (10) 3 ½" wide strips |
| Second Border | 2¾ yds | (12) 7 ½" wide strips |
| Backing | 9½ yds | Cut 3 equal pieces & seam |
| Bonded Batting | 110" x 110" | |
| Binding | 1⅓ yds | (11) 3 ½" wide strips |

# Sewing the Blocks

## Making the Rows

The Block has five horizontal rows, each with different fabric arrangements. **The background pieces are oversized for trimming purposes.**

### Row One

1. Stack and lay out the number of 2 ½" wide A and B strips as listed in the table to the left for your size quilt.

| Quilt | Amt. |
|---|---|
| **Baby** | 1 |
| **Lap** | 2 |
| **Twin** | 3 |
| **Double** | 3 |
| **Queen** | 4 |
| **King** | 6 |

2. Flip strip B onto A. Sew ¼" seam allowance.

    Use ¼" seam allowance accurately and consistently.

    Sew 15 stitches to the inch.

### Larger than Baby size:

Do not remove strip from machine or clip threads. Butt the next pair of A/B strips, and assembly-line sew until all stacked A and B strips are used.

3. Set the seam and direct the seam allowance under A.

   Seam allowances are pressed in specific directions under strips so that the seams will interlock on the finished block.

   Lay sewn strip, closed, on ironing board with A on top.

   Press stitching to "set the seam."

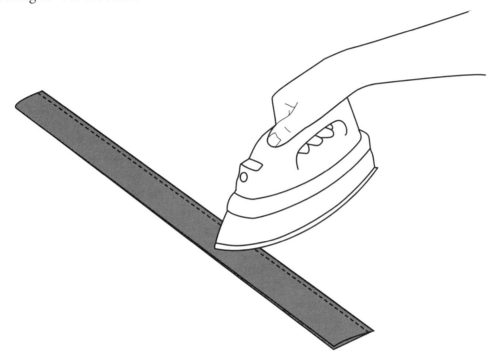

Lift A and press toward seam line to "direct the seam allowance under A." Make sure there are no folds at the seam line.

Stack the A/B's.

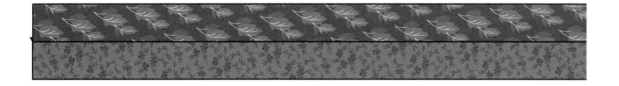

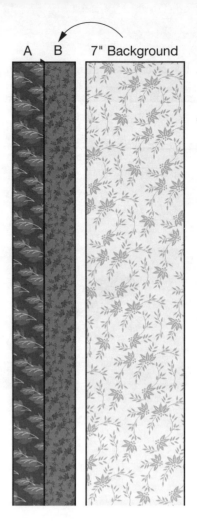

4.  Stack and lay out an equal number of 7"
    wide Background strips with stacked A/B
    strips.  Place the B side next to the
    Background stack.

5.  Flip Background piece onto A/B right
    sides together.

    Sew.  Assembly-line sew if more than one.

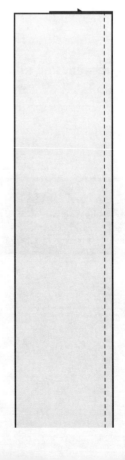

6. Place sewn strip, closed, on ironing board with A/B on top. Press on stitching to "set the seam."

   Lift A/B and press toward seam line to "direct the seam allowance under B." Make sure there are no folds at the seam line.

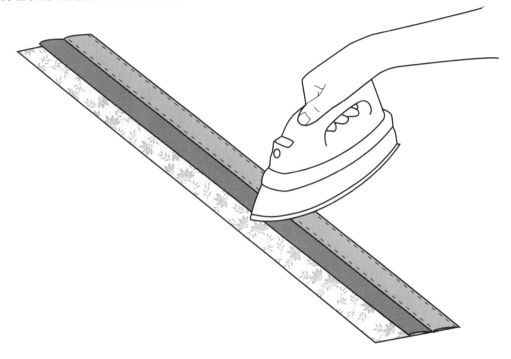

7. Label, stack, and put aside Rows One.

   All seams are pressed toward A.

### Row Two

1.  Stack and lay out the number of 2 ½"
    wide B and C strips as listed in the table
    to the left for your size quilt.

| Quilt | Amt. |
| --- | --- |
| **Baby** | **1** |
| **Lap** | **2** |
| **Twin** | **3** |
| **Double** | **3** |
| **Queen** | **4** |
| **King** | **6** |

2.  Flip strip C onto B.  Sew.

    Assembly-line sew if more than one.

3.  Lay sewn strip on ironing board with C on top. Press stitching to set the seam. Lift C and press toward seam line to direct seam allowance under C. Stack.

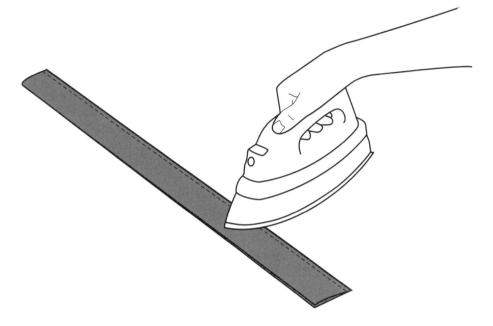

4.  Stack and lay out an equal number of D strips with stack of B/C strips. Place the C side next to the D stack.

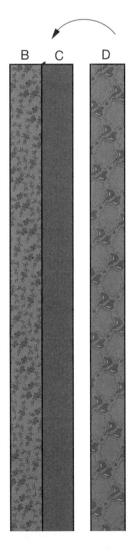

5. Flip D strip onto C.  Sew.

   Assembly-line sew if more than one.

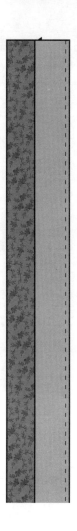

6. Set the seam with D on top, and direct seam allowance under D.  Stack.

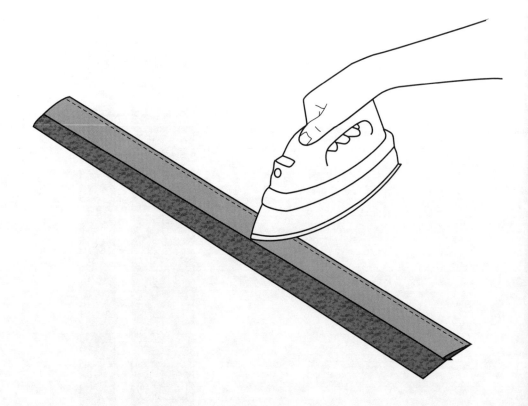

7. Stack and lay out an equal number of 5"
   wide Background strips with stacked
   B/C/D strips.  Place D side next to
   Background stack.

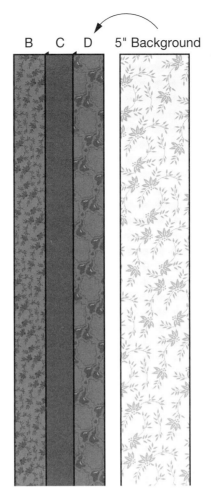

8. Flip Background piece onto B/C/D. Sew.

   Assembly-line sew if more than one.

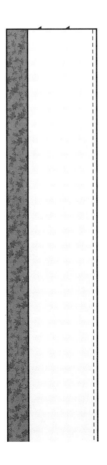

9. Set the seam with the Background on top, and direct seam allowance under Background.

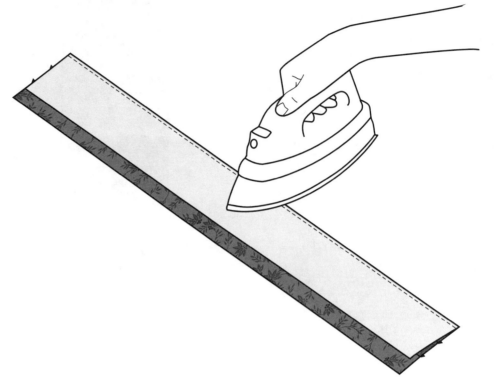

10. Label, stack, and put aside Rows Two.

   All seams are pressed toward Background.

## Row Three

1. Stack and lay out the number of 3" wide Background strips and 2 ½" wide D strips as listed in the table to the right for your size quilt.

3" Background   D

| Quilt | Amt. |
|---|---|
| **Baby** | **1** |
| **Lap** | **2** |
| **Twin** | **3** |
| **Double** | **3** |
| **Queen** | **4** |
| **King** | **6** |

2. Flip strip D onto Background. Sew.

   Assembly-line sew if more than one.

3. Set the seam with Background on top, and direct seam allowance under Background. Stack.

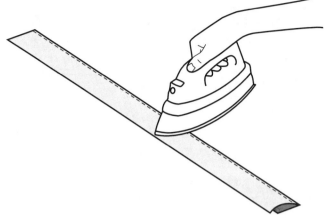

4. Stack and lay out an equal number of E strips with stack of Background/D strips. Place the D side next to the E stack.

5. Flip E strip onto D. Sew.

   Assembly-line sew if more than one.

6. Set the seam with Background/D on top, and direct seam allowance under D. Stack.

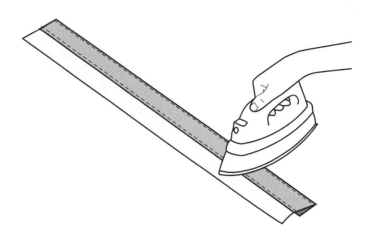

7. Stack and lay out an equal number of F strips with stacked Background/D/E strips. Place E side next to F stack.

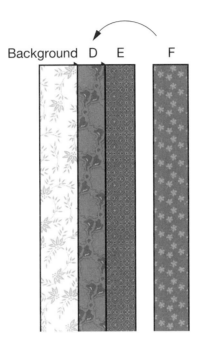

8. Flip F strip onto E. Sew.

Assembly-line sew if more than one.

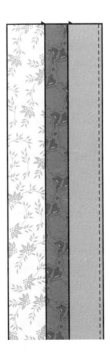

9. Set the seam with Background/D/E on top, and direct seam allowance under E. Stack.

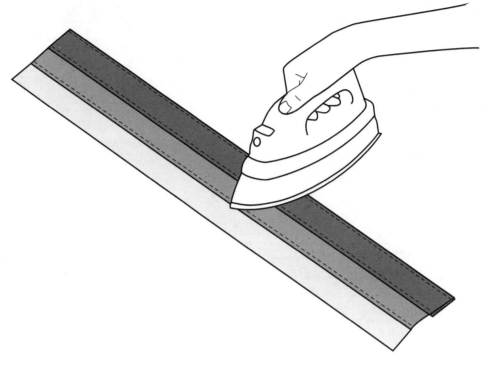

10. Stack and lay out an equal number of 3" wide Background strips with Background/D/E/F stack. Place F side next to Background stack.

Background   D   E   F   3" Background

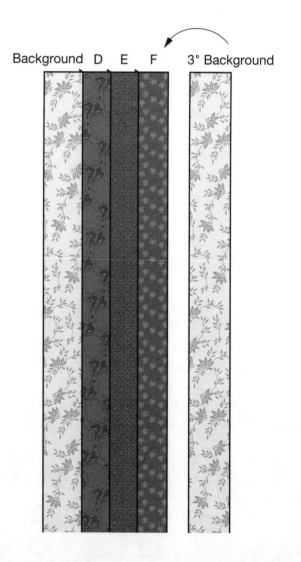

11. Flip Background strip onto F. Sew. Assembly-line sew if more than one.

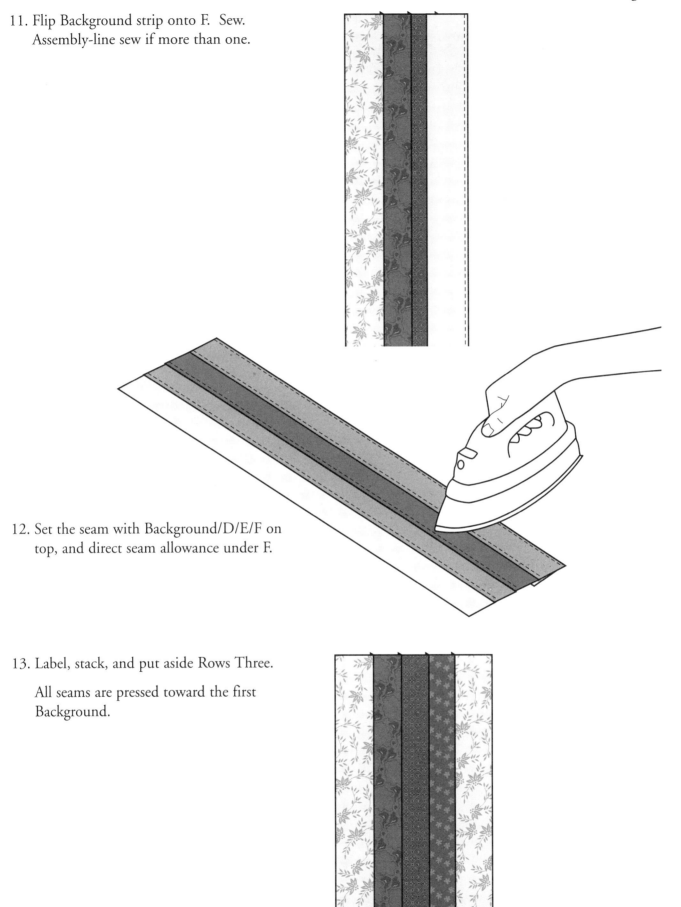

12. Set the seam with Background/D/E/F on top, and direct seam allowance under F.

13. Label, stack, and put aside Rows Three.

   All seams are pressed toward the first Background.

## Row Four

| Quilt | Amt. |
|--------|------|
| **Baby** | 1 |
| **Lap** | 2 |
| **Twin** | 3 |
| **Double** | 3 |
| **Queen** | 4 |
| **King** | 6 |

1. Stack and lay out the number of 5" wide Background strips and 2 ½" wide F strips as listed in the table to the left for your size quilt.

2. Flip strip F onto Background. Sew. Assembly-line sew if more than one.

3. Set the seam with F on top, and direct seam allowance under F. Stack.

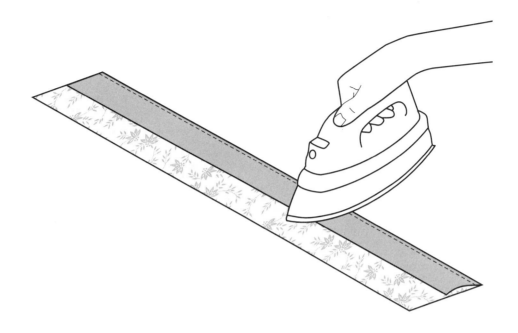

4. Stack and lay out an equal number of G strips with stack of Background/F strips. Place the F side next to the G stack.

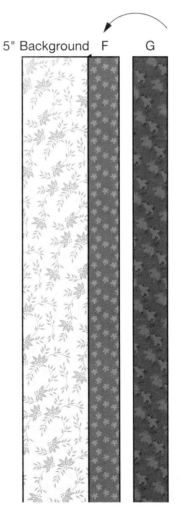

5" Background   F        G

5.  Flip G onto F.  Sew.

    Assembly-line sew if more than one.

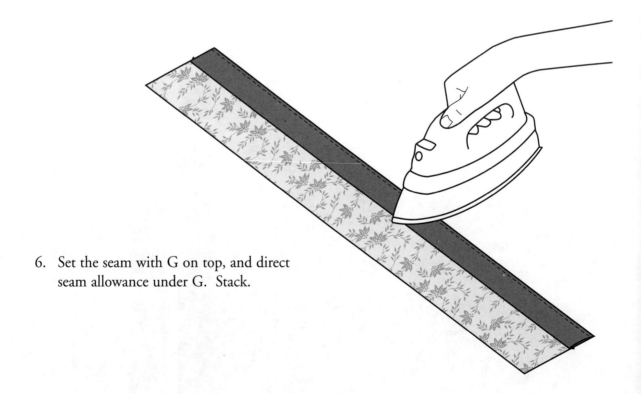

6.  Set the seam with G on top, and direct
    seam allowance under G.  Stack.

7. Stack and lay out an equal number of H strips with stacked Background/F/G strips. Place G side next to H stack.

5" Background    F    G      H

8. Flip H onto G. Sew.

   Assembly-line sew if more than one.

9. Set the seam with the H on top, and direct seam allowance under H.

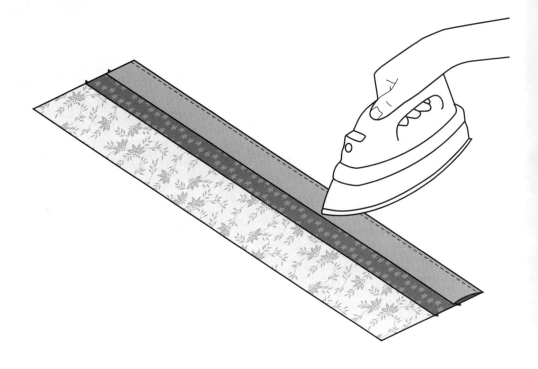

10. Label, stack, and put aside Rows Four.

    All seams are pressed toward H.

## Row Five

1. Stack and lay out the number of 7" wide Background strips and 2 ½" wide H strips as listed in the table to the right for your size quilt.

7" Background      H

| Quilt | Amt. |
|---|---|
| Baby | 1 |
| Lap | 2 |
| Twin | 3 |
| Double | 3 |
| Queen | 4 |
| King | 6 |

2. Flip strip H onto Background. Sew. Assembly-line sew if more than one.

3. Set the seam with the Background on top, and direct seam allowance under the Background. Stack.

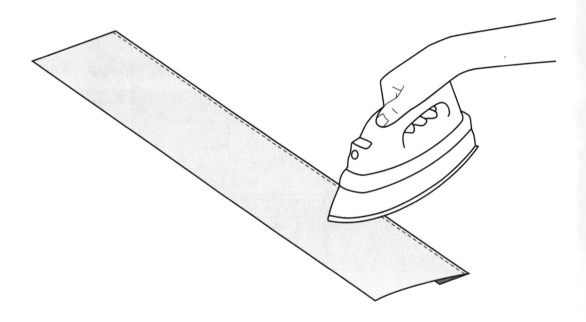

4. Stack and lay out an equal number of I strips with stack of Background/H strips. Place the H side next to the I stack.

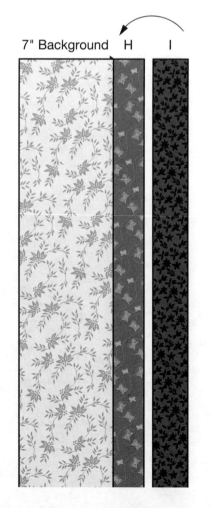

7" Background  H  I

5. Flip I onto H. Sew.

   Assembly-line sew if more than one.

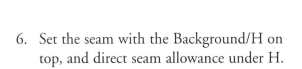

6. Set the seam with the Background/H on top, and direct seam allowance under H.

7. Label, stack, and put aside Rows Five.

   All seams are pressed toward Background.

## Cutting and Sewing Rows One and Two

Check the grid lines of your cutting mat against your ruler. If the inches match, you may use the cutting mat grid lines to measure.

1.  Lay **Row Two** right side up on cutting mat with B across the top. Align with grid. Extend the selvages of the left end beyond the "0" grid line.

2.  Lay **Row One** wrong side up on Row Two with A across the top.

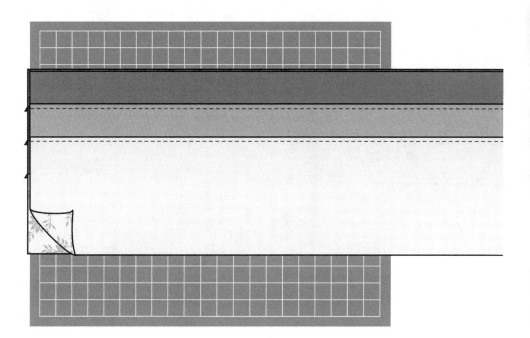

3.  Smooth the layers together with your hands, locking the seams. The Background edges along the bottom will not be even.

4.  Lay the 6" x 12" ruler on the "0" grid line and rotary trim the left end even.

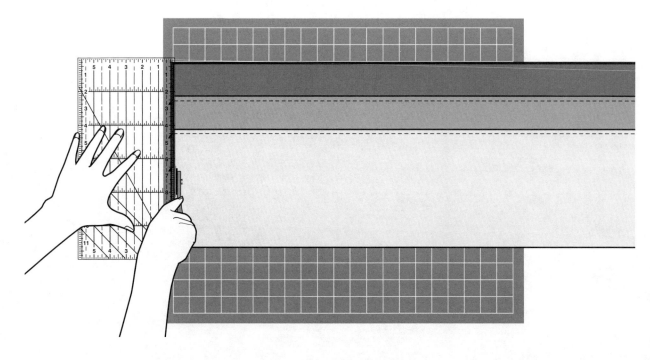

5. Lift and move ruler. Do not slide it on the strips. Measure 2 ½" from cut end. Place ruler parallel with grid lines for a straight cut.

   Rotary cut layered pair. Lift and move ruler.

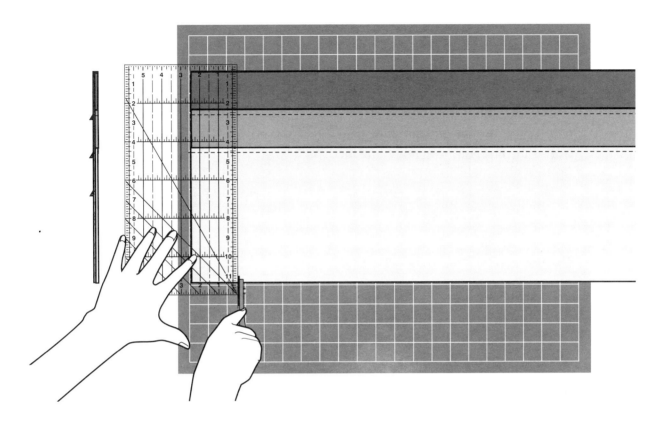

6. Repeat cutting the number of 2 ½" wide layered pairs as listed in the table to the right for your size quilt.

   Lay cut pieces on a 12 ½" Square Up ruler to carry to the machine.

| Quilt | Pairs |
|--------|-------|
| **Baby** | **16** |
| **Lap** | **24** |
| **Twin** | **40** |
| **Double** | **48** |
| **Queen** | **63** |
| **King** | **81** |

7. Pick up a layered pair with A at the top. Open and check to see that B is underneath. "Wiggle match" the seams to meet. Pin if desired. Sew a ¼" seam allowance. Do not remove from machine or cut threads, but open pair to see if seams meet.

8. Pick up next layered pair and butt them against the first pair. Assembly-line sew all Rows One and Two.

9. Cut connecting threads.

10. Lay on ironing board with **Row One** on top. Press to set the seam, and direct the seam allowance under Row One.

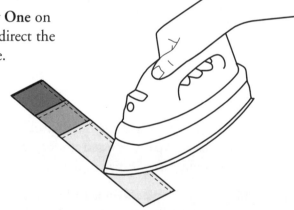

11. Stack and set aside.

# Cutting and Sewing Rows Three and Four

| Quilt | Pairs |
|--------|-------|
| Baby | 16 |
| Lap | 24 |
| Twin | 40 |
| Double | 48 |
| Queen | 63 |
| King | 81 |

1. Lay **Row Three** right side up on cutting mat with the Background/F edge across the top. Align with grid. Extend the selvages of the left end beyond the "0" grid line.

2. Lay **Row Four** wrong side up on Row Three with H across the top.

3. Repeat as with Rows One and Two. Trim end. Cut the number of 2 ½" wide layered pairs as listed in the table for your size quilt.

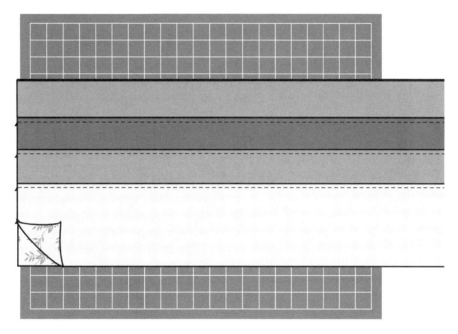

4. Assembly-line sew pairs.

5. Set the seam with **Row Three** on top, and direct seam under Row Three.

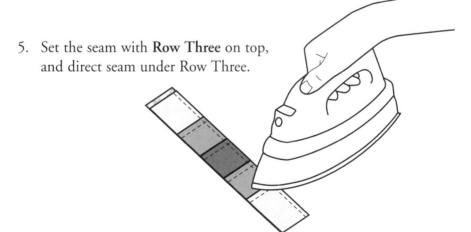

6. Stack.

# Sewing Rows Three/Four to One/Two

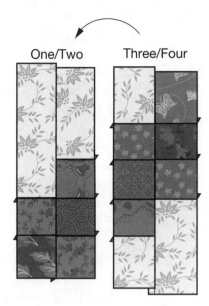

One/Two    Three/Four

1. Lay out stacks forming pattern. Make sure Row Three is next to Row Two.

2. Flip Rows Three/Four onto One/Two. "Wiggle match" the seams. The ends do not match. The under seams are pointed away from you and will tend to fold down. Sew carefully as you approach a match point. Lift the pair slightly to tuck the under seam in place. Assembly-line sew.

3. Set the seam with Rows One/Two on top, and direct the seam under Row Two.

4. Stack.

# Adding Row Five

1. Trim selvages and cut Row Five strips into the number of 2 ½" wide pieces as listed in the table to the right for your size quilt. Cut single or double layers as your prefer.

| Quilt | Amt. |
|---|---|
| **Baby** | 16 |
| **Lap** | 24 |
| **Twin** | 40 |
| **Double** | 48 |
| **Queen** | 63 |
| **King** | 81 |

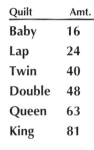

2. Stack Row Five pieces with stacked Rows One/Two/Three/Four.

   Make sure the pattern is established with the Row Four side next to Row Five. Flip the I end of Row Five onto the sewn rows.

3. Sew carefully to the match points, pushing under seam allowances in place. Assembly-line sew.

4. Set the seam with sewn rows on top, and direct the seam allowance under Row 4. Stack.

# Squaring Up the Blocks

The blocks have been constructed to have uneven edges. The uneven edges will be trimmed while centering the Square Up ruler on the block.

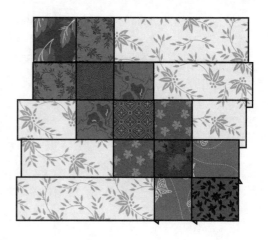

## Find the Average Size of Your Blocks

Ideally the blocks are 10 ½" square, but they probably will be smaller. Use the 12 ½" Square Up ruler to measure several blocks to find the average size. Measure from one horizontal edge to the other.

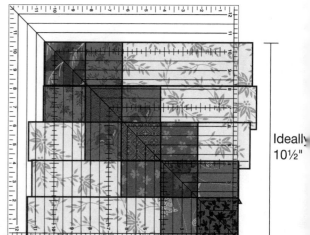

Ideally 10½"

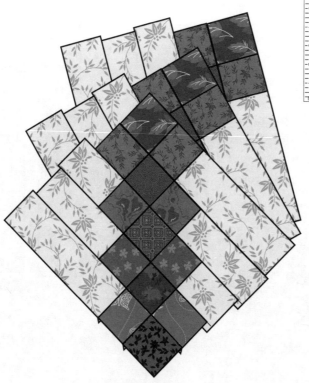

## Trimming the Blocks to the Average Size

1. Measure from one horizontal edge to the other. These are the edges that should be even, while the vertical edges should be uneven. Find the average measurement after measuring a fair amount of your blocks.

2. Place the Square Up ruler with the average measurement across the bottom and top of the block. Be sure that the diagonal line runs through the center of the chain. Trim off the uneven edges to the right side of the ruler.

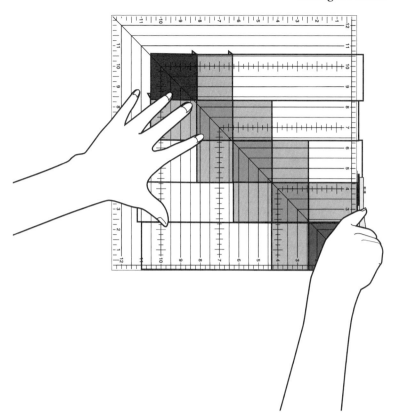

3. Take the righthand top corner and turn it so that it is now in the bottom lefthand position. Again place your ruler so that it runs evenly across the bottom of your block with your block measurement. Be sure that the diagonal line runs through the center of the chain. Trim off the uneven edges to the right side of the ruler.

4. Repeat for all blocks.

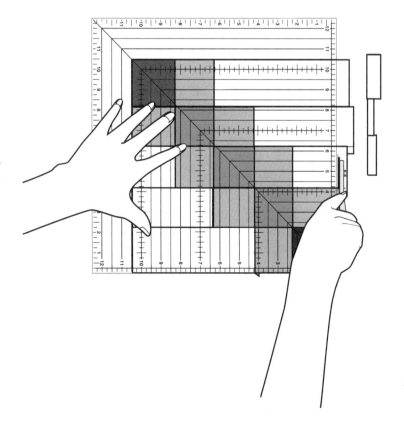

# Sewing the Top Together

Row 1   Row 2   Row 3   Row 4

| Blocks | Across | Down |
|--------|--------|------|
| **Baby** | 4 | 4 |
| **Lap** | 4 | 6 |
| **Twin** | 5 | 8 |
| **Double** | 6 | 8 |
| **Queen** | 7 | 9 |
| **King** | 9 | 9 |

1. Lay out the blocks following the number listed in the table for your quilt size.

2. Flip the second vertical row right sides together onto the first vertical row.

3. Pick up and stack the pairs of blocks starting at the top. The pair at the top will be on top of the stack.

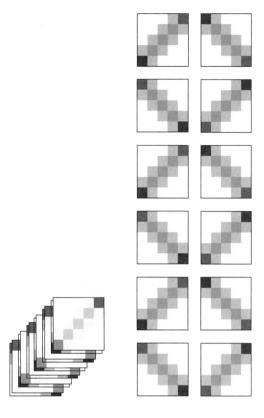

4. Stack each of the vertical rows from the bottom to the top, having the top block on the top of the stack each time.

Write the row number on a piece of paper and pin it through all thicknesses of fabric.

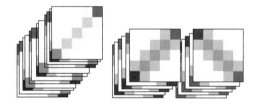

# Sewing the Vertical Seams

Start with the stack of paired blocks. Lay the stack of paired blocks next to your sewing machine. Be careful not to turn the stack.

1. Pick up top paired blocks.

   Stitch down about ½" to anchor the two together.

   Match, pin, or fingerpin by squeezing tightly the rows of the block as they come together.

   Stitch and fingerpin the next row. Stitch.

2. Do not cut the threads or lift the presser foot.

   Pick up your next pair of blocks. Butt them right behind the first two.

   Anchor the two with ½" of stitching. Fingerpin the rows and corners of the blocks. Ease the two blocks to fit. Stitch.

3. In the same manner, continue butting on your next pair.

   Butt and stitch all the blocks until the blocks of Row 1 and Row 2 are completed.

   Do not cut the blocks apart.

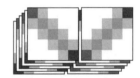

## Adding the Third Vertical Row

Place the stacked 3rd vertical row of blocks next to your sewing machine. Be careful not to turn the stack.

1. Open the chained pairs of blocks. Examine them to make sure they follow the arrangement layout.

   Place the block at the top of the third vertical row right sides together to the next block.

   Ease and stitch the two to meet, matching rows and corners.

   Pin if needed.

   Butt, ease and stitch the second block in the third vertical row.

2. Continue sewing all blocks in all vertical rows in the same manner.

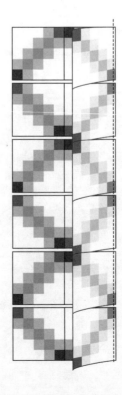

Do not clip the threads holding the blocks together.

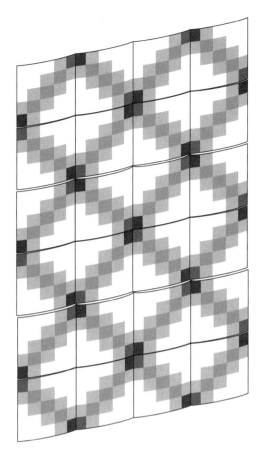

*Example illustration… Yours may look different according to the size of your quilt.*

# Sewing the Horizontal Rows

1.  Flip the top row down onto the second row with right sides together. Match, ease, and stitch the rows and blocks to meet. Where the two blocks are joined by a thread, match the seam carefully. Push the vertical seam allowances in opposite directions.

2.  Stitch all horizontal rows in the same manner, keeping the vertical seam allowances pushed in the same direction.

3.  Press the quilt top.

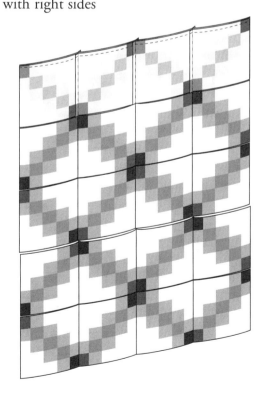

# Adding the Borders

### Designing the Borders

Suggested border yardage and border examples are given for each quilt. However, you may wish to custom design the borders by changing the widths of the strips. This may change backing and batting yardages.

When custom fitting the quilt, lay the top on your bed before adding the borders and backing. Measure to find how much border is needed to get the fit you want. Keep in mind that the quilt will "shrink" approximately 3" in the length and width after tying, "stitching in the ditch" and/or machine quilting.

### Piecing the Border Strips

1. Stack and square off the ends of each strip, trimming away the selvage edges.

2. Seam the strips of each fabric into long pieces by assembly-line sewing. Lay the first strip right side up. Lay the second strip right sides to it. Backstitch, stitch the short ends together, and backstitch again.

   Take the strip on the top and fold it so the right side is up.

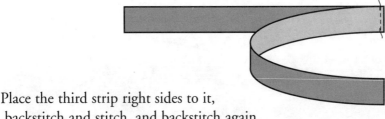

   Place the third strip right sides to it,
   backstitch and stitch, and backstitch again.

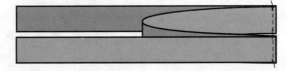

   Continue assembly-line sewing all the short ends together into long pieces for each fabric.

   Clip the threads holding the strips together.

3. Press seams to one side.

## Sewing the Borders to the Quilt Top

1. Measure down the center of the quilt to find the length. Cut two side strips that measurement plus two inches.

2. Right sides together, match and pin the center of the strips to the center of the sides. Extend one inch of strip on each end. Be sure to pin at the ends and intermittently along the sides. Sew with the quilt on top.

3. "Set and direct the seams," pressing toward the border.

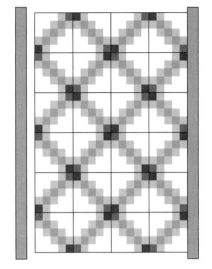

4. Square the ends even with the top and bottom edges of the quilt.

5. Measure the width across the center including newly added borders. Cut two strips that measurement plus two inches.

6. Right sides together, match and pin the center of the strips to the center of the top and bottom edges of the quilt. Extend one inch of strip on each end. Pin at the ends and every three inches along the border. Sew with the quilt on top.

7. "Set and direct the seams," pressing toward that border.

8. Square the ends even with the side borders.

9. Repeat these steps for additional borders.

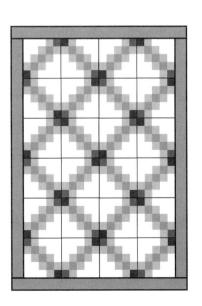

# Finishing the Quilt

*There are two options in finishing your quilt. They are Machine Quilting with a Binding or a Quick Turn and Tie. Quick Turn and Tie is the easier method. Option of the Machine Quilting finish is found on page 58.*

## Option of Quick Turn and Tie

The Quick Turn method is the easier and faster way to finish the quilt. Thick batting is "rolled" into the middle of the quilt, and the layers are held together with ties of embroidery floss. Borders may be "stitched in the ditch" for additional dimension. For this stitching, use a walking foot sewing machine attachment to keep the layers feeding evenly. Use invisible thread in the top and a regular bobbin thread to match the backing.

### Sewing and Layering a Quick Turn

1. Piece backing yardage together for larger size quilts.

2. Lay out the oversized backing fabric, right side up, on a large table or floor. Clamp to the table with binder clips or tape to the floor.

3. Lay the quilt top on the backing fabric with the right sides together. Stretch and smooth the top. Pin. Trim away excess backing. The quilt top, batting and backing should be the same size.

4. Use a ¼" seam allowance and sew around the four sides of the quilt, leaving a 24" opening in the middle of one long side. Do not turn the quilt right side out.

5. Lay the quilt on top of the batting. Smooth and trim the batting to the same size as the quilt top

   To assure that the batting stays out to the edges, whipstitch the batting to the ¼" seam allowance around the outside edge of the quilt.

## Turning the Quilt Top

1. If you are working with a group, station the people at the corners of the quilt. If working alone, start in one corner opposite the opening.

*One person can turn the quilt alone, but it's helpful if two or three others can help. Read this whole section before beginning. If several people are helping, all should roll toward the opening. If only one is doing the rolling, use a knee to hold down one corner while stretching over to the corners.*

2. Roll the corners and sides tightly to keep the batting in place as you roll toward the opening.

3. Open up the opening over this huge wad of fabric and batting, and pop the quilt right side out through the hole.

4. Unroll carefully with the layers together.

5. Lay the quilt flat on the floor or on a very large table. Work out all wrinkles and bumps by stationing two people opposite each other around the quilt. Have each person grasp the edge and tug the quilt in opposite directions.

   You can also relocate any batting by reaching inside the quilt through the opening with a yardstick. Hold the edges and shake the batting into place if necessary.

6. Slipstitch the opening shut.

## Finishing the Quick Turn Quilt

You may choose to tie your entire quilt, or machine quilt by "stitching in the ditch" around the borders and tying in the blocks. A quilt with thick batting is difficult to machine quilt the blocks because it is hard to get all the rolled thickness to fit through the keyhole of the sewing machine. You can, however, machine quilt by "stitching in the ditch" along the border seams.

## Tying the Quilt

1. Thread a large-eyed curved needle with six strands of embroidery floss, crochet thread, or other thread of your choice.

2. Plan where you want your ties placed, about 5 to 8 inches apart. Do not tie in the borders if you wish to "stitch in the ditch."

3. Starting in the center of the quilt and working to the outside, take a ¼" stitch through all thicknesses at the points you wish to tie. Draw the curved needle along to each point, going in and out, and replacing the tying material as needed.

4. Clip all the stitches midway.

5. Tie the strands into surgeon's knots by taking the strand on the right and wrapping it twice. Pull the knot tight. Take the strand on the left, wrap it twice, and pull the knot tight.

6. Clip the strands so they are ½" to 1" long.

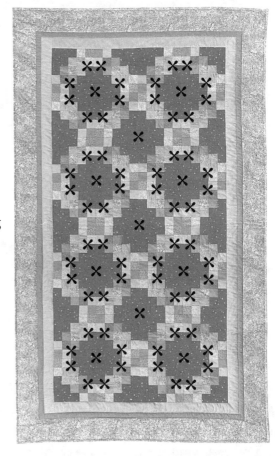

## "Stitching in the Ditch"

For more dimensional borders, you may choose to "stitch in the ditch" rather than tie the borders. A walking foot or even-feed foot sewing machine attachment is necessary to keep the three layers feeding at the same rate.

Change your stitch length to 10 stitches per inch or #3 setting. Match your bobbin color of thread to your backing color. Loosen the top tension and thread with the soft nylon invisible thread.

1. Safety pin the length of the borders.

2. Place the needle in the depth of the seam and pull up the bobbin thread. Lock the beginning and ending of the quilting line by backstitching ½". Run your hand underneath to feel for puckers. Grasp the quilt with your left hand above the sewing machine, and grasp the quilt ten inches below the walking foot with your right hand as you stitch. If you need to ease in the top fabric, feed the quilt through the machine by pushing the layers of fabric and batting forward underneath the walking foot.

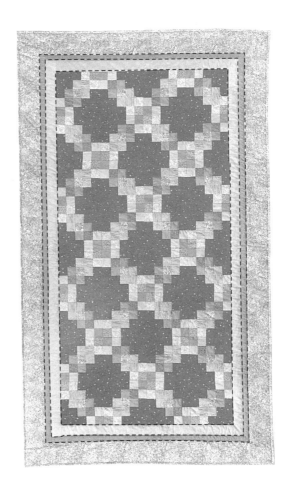

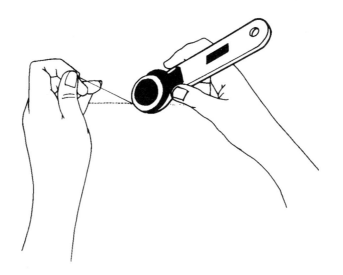

*If puckering occurs, remove stitching by grasping the bobbin thread with a pin or tweezers and pull gently to expose the invisible thread. Touch the invisible thread stitches with the rotary cutter blade as you pull the bobbin thread free from the quilt.*

# Option of Machine Quilting with a Binding Finish

## Marking the Quilt

Decide where you want the quilting lines. You may mark the quilt using the "Follow Your Dream" stencil (page 61) in the open areas, or mark diagonal sewing lines through the chain. Both designs can be used in the same quilt.

You can use the 6" by 24" ruler and your favorite marker to draw the lines for machine quilting. Be sure that you test whatever marker you choose on a scrap piece of material to be sure that you can remove the marks from your quilt.

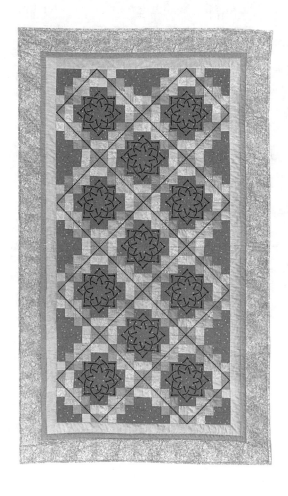

## Layering Quilt Top with Backing and Batting

1. Piece the backing yardage together for larger size quilts.

2. Stretch out the backing right side down on a large floor area or table. Tape down on a floor area or clamp onto a table with large binder clips.

3. Place and smooth out the batting on top. Lay the quilt top right side up and centered on top of the batting. Completely smooth and stretch all layers until they are flat. Re-tape or clip securely. The backing and batting should extend at least 2" on all sides.

## Quick and Easy Safety Pinning

Place safety pins throughout the quilt away from the marked quilting lines. Begin pinning in the center and work to the outside, spacing them every 5".

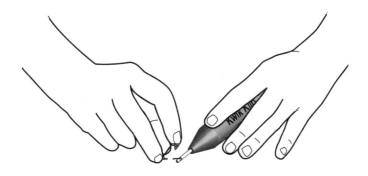

*Grasp the opened pin in your right hand and the pinning tool in your left hand. Push the pin through the three layers, and bring the tip of the pin back out. Catch the tip in the groove of the tool and allow point to extend far enough to push pin closure down.*

## Machine Quilting the Straight Lines

Use a walking foot attachment for straight line quilting. Use invisible thread in the top of your machine and regular thread in the bobbin to match the backing. Loosen the top tension, and lengthen your stitch to 8 - 10 stitches per inch, or a #3 or #4 setting.

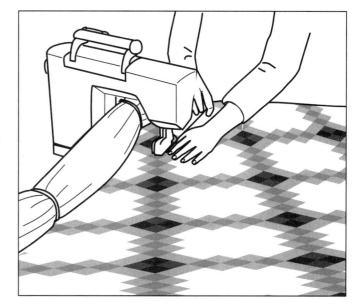

1. Roll the quilt tightly from the outside edge in toward middle. Hold this roll with metal bicycle clips or pins.

2. Slide this roll into the keyhole of the sewing machine.

3. Place the needle in the depth of the seam and pull up the bobbin thread. Lock your thread with ½" of tiny stitches when you begin and end your sewing line. Run your hand underneath to feel for puckers.

4. Place your hands flat on both sides of the needle. Keep the quilt area flat and tight. If you need to ease in the top fabric, feed the quilt through the machine by pushing the layers of fabric and batting forward underneath the walking foot.

If puckering occurs, remove the stitching by grasping the bobbin thread with a pin or tweezers and pull gently to expose the invisible thread. Touch the invisible thread stitches with the rotary cutter blade as you pull the bobbin thread free from the quilt. Re-sew.

5. Unroll, roll, and machine quilt on all lines, sewing the length or width or diagonal of the quilt.

If outline stitching, use the edge of the walking foot as a guide. At corners, pivot with the needle in the quilt.

## Free Motion Quilting

The "Follow Your Dream" stencil was designed by Hari Walner for continuous machine quilting. You may choose to trace the illustrations on page 61 or use a purchased stencil available from Quilt in a Day.

This is a more advanced method of machine quilting using a darning foot attachment or a spring needle. You have the freedom to stitch forward, backward, and to the side without the use of a presser foot or feed dogs. However, this method requires practice.

Refer to your instruction manual for how to darn with your machine. You will need to use a darning foot and drop or cover the feed dogs with a plate.

No stitch length is required as you control the length of the stitch. Lower the speed of your machine and use "needle down" position, if possible. Use a fine needle and a little hole throat plate if available. Use invisible thread or regular thread in the top, and thread to match your backing in the bobbin.

Before you begin to sew, study your quilting design to determine the best direction for free motion quilting.

1.  At the starting point, put the presser foot down. The quilt should move freely under the darning foot. Lower the needle and bring up the bobbin thread. Hold both threads. Move the fabric very slowly to lock the line with tiny stitches. Clip off the threads.

2.  With your eyes watching the line ahead of the needle, and both hands grasping the fabric and acting as a quilting hoop, move the fabric in a steady motion while the machine is running at a constant speed. Do not move the fabric fast as this will result in large stitches and may even break the needle.

3.  The size of the stitch is controlled by the speed of the movement. Keep the top of the block in the same position by moving the fabric from side to side and forward and backward.

4.  When finishing a line, lock with tiny stitches and clip thread at the top. Tug bobbin thread slightly and cut.

Start

## Adding the Binding

Use a walking foot attachment and regular thread on top and in the bobbin to match the binding. Use 10 stitches per inch, or #3 setting.

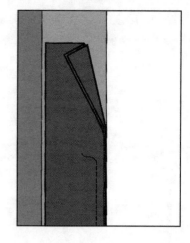

1. Square ends. Sew strips into one long piece by assembly-line sewing.

2. Press the binding strip in half lengthwise with right sides out.

3. Line up the raw edges of the folded binding with the raw edge of the quilt top at the middle of one side. Begin sewing 4" from the end of the binding.

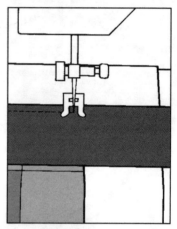

4. At the corner, stop the stitching ¼" from the edge with the needle in the fabric. Raise the presser foot and turn the quilt to the next side. Put the foot back down.

5. Sew backwards ¼" to the edge of the binding, raise the foot, and pull the quilt forward slightly.

6. Fold the binding strip straight up on the diagonal. Fingerpress in the diagonal fold.

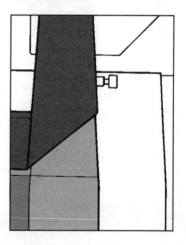

7. Fold the binding strip straight down with the diagonal fold underneath. Line up the top of the fold with the raw edge of the binding underneath. Begin sewing from the corner. Continue sewing and mitering the corners around the outside of the quilt.

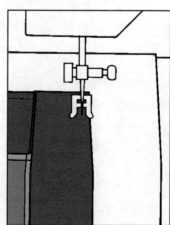

8.  Stop sewing 4" from where the ends will overlap. Line up the two ends of binding. Trim the excess with a ½" overlap.

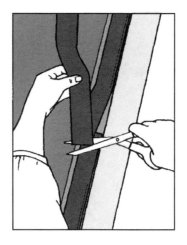

9.  Open out the folded ends and pin right sides together. Sew a ¼" seam.

10. Continue to sew the binding in place.

11. Trim the batting and backing up to the raw edges of the binding.

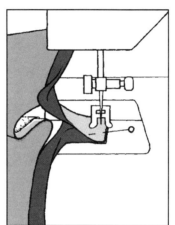

12. Fold the binding to the backside of the quilt. Pin in place so that the folded edge on the binding covers the stitching line. Tuck in the excess fabric at each miter on the diagonal.

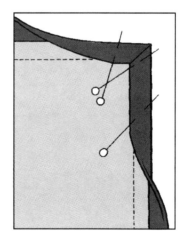

13. From the right side, "stitch in the ditch" using invisible thread on the right side, and a bobbin thread to match the binding on the back side. Catch the folded edge of the binding on the back side with the stitching.

    *Optional: Hand slip-stitch the binding in place.*

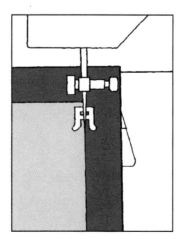

# Index